YOU CHOOSE

CAN YOU ESCAPE A HAUNTED CEMETERY?

AN INTERACTIVE PARANORMAL ADVENTURE

BY AILYNN COLLINS

Published by Capstone Press, an imprint of Capstone
1710 Roe Crest Drive, North Mankato, Minnesota 56003
capstonepub.com

Copyright © 2025 by Capstone. All rights reserved. No part of this publication may be reproduced in whole or in part, or stored in a retrieval system, or transmitted in any form or by any means, electronic, mechanical, photocopying, recording, or otherwise, without written permission of the publisher.

Library of Congress Cataloging-in-Publication Data is available on the Library of Congress website.

ISBN: 9781669069232 (hardcover)
ISBN: 9781669069201 (paperback)
ISBN: 9781669069218 (ebook PDF)

Summary: Readers explore haunted cemeteries around the world and experience paranormal activity inspired by reports from real people.

Editorial Credits
Editor: Mandy Robbins; Designer: Dina Her; Media Researcher: Jo Miller: Production Specialist: Tori Abraham

Photo Credits
Getty Images: Zoran_Photo, 16; Shutterstock: Alexander Beker, 49, 107, Arcady, 77, BaLL LunLa, 38, brunocoelho, 46, clivewa, 82, Evgrafova Svetlana, 24, Fer Gregory, Cover (graveyard), Francesco Bonino, 72, Garrett Photos, 106, GogOfVector, 6, HASPhotos, 79, Helen Hotson, 102, Jakub Krechowicz, 58, Jeff Thrower, 64, Juiced Up Media, 42, 104, Leigh J, 10, Limnophila, Cover (ghost silhouette), Madrugada Verde, 94, Manuel Ascanio, 53, Melinda Nagy, 87, Raggedstone, 69, reptiles4all, 34, Roberto La Rosa, 92, Scott A . Burns, 27, TravellingFatman, 62

Design Elements
Shutterstock: Nik Merkulov, Olha Nion

Any additional websites and resources referenced in this book are not maintained, authorized, or sponsored by Capstone. All product and company names are trademarks™ or registered® trademarks of their respective holders.

Printed and bound in China. 6274

TABLE OF CONTENTS

INTRODUCTION
ABOUT YOUR ADVENTURE..................5

CHAPTER 1
A TRIP TO REMEMBER....................7

CHAPTER 2
ST. LOUIS CEMETERY NUMBER ONE........11

CHAPTER 3
AOYAMA CEMETERY.....................39

CHAPTER 4
GREYFRIARS KIRKYARD..................73

CHAPTER 5
GHOSTS IN GRAVEYARDS...............103

MORE GHOSTLY ENCOUNTERS.............106
OTHER PATHS TO EXPLORE..............108
GLOSSARY............................109
BIBLIOGRAPHY........................110
READ MORE...........................111
INTERNET SITES......................111
ABOUT THE AUTHOR....................112

INTRODUCTION
ABOUT YOUR ADVENTURE

Cemeteries are where the dead are put to rest, but are they all resting? Face eerie experiences reported by real people in three famous cemeteries. Can you escape a haunted cemetery?

Chapter One sets the scene. Then you choose which path to read. Follow the directions at the bottom of the page. Your decisions will change your outcome. After you finish one path, go back and read the others for new perspectives and more adventures.

Turn the page to begin your adventure.

CHAPTER 1
A TRIP TO REMEMBER

Ever since you can remember, you've loved making up scary ghost stories. Whether it was camping in the backyard or under a blanket fort in your room, you and your sister told each other stories about ghosts in graveyards. The chills these tales give you made you both giggle with delight.

So, when your parents said the options for this year's spring break trip are all cities that have famous cemeteries, you cannot contain your excitement. The hardest part is that you have to choose between New Orleans, Tokyo, Japan, or Edinburgh, Scotland.

Turn the page.

New Orleans is the home of St. Louis Cemetery Number One. It's one of the oldest cemeteries in the United States and is rumored to be haunted. Your sister is in college now, and she would be able to meet you there.

Your Uncle Roger and Aunt Therese are ghost hunters in Tokyo, Japan. If you visit them, you can investigate the Aoyama Cemetery with them. It is the most haunted cemetery in Japan.

You could also choose to visit your cousin Angus in Scotland. He lives near Greyfriars Kirkyard in Edinburgh. It's the most haunted cemetery in the entire world.

It's hard to choose. Each place has fascinated you for a long time. Where will you go?

- To go to New Orleans, turn to page 11.
- To visit Uncle Roger and Aunt Therese in Tokyo, turn to page 39.
- To visit to your cousin in Scotland, turn to page 73.

CHAPTER 2
ST. LOUIS CEMETERY NUMBER ONE

You can't pass up the opportunity to tour a haunted cemetery with your sister. Your parents don't like ghosts. They decide to wait in a café across the street while you and your sister join the tour.

At sunset, the tour group gathers in front of the café. Your guide, Misette, is a friendly woman. You follow her across the street to a tall, white wall. Behind it is the cemetery.

"Sadly, people have not been respectful of the graves here," Misette says. "The only way to get inside now is with a tour group. But we often experience ghostly activity."

Turn the page.

You and your sister grasp hands and look at each other with excitement. You enter the cemetery through a narrow gateway. Hundreds of tombs stand closely crammed together. Many of them are taller than you. Some look like they're falling apart. Several tombs are protected by iron fences. A few have flowering bushes planted around them. The pathways between tombs are smooth and paved. Oddly, the cemetery feels neat and untidy at the same time.

"It's said that only the ghosts know their way around here." Misette lowers her voice. "Don't get lost. Not all the ghosts here are friendly."

"It doesn't look scary to me," you whisper to your sister.

Misette pauses between paths. "Welcome to St. Louis Cemetery Number One," she says.

"This is the oldest grave site in New Orleans. It was opened in 1789 by the Spanish and holds over 700 tombs. We believe more than 100,000 people are buried here."

"How is there enough room for so many dead?" you ask.

"Several tombs hold generations of families," Misette answers.

She points to the brick section on the top of a smooth white tomb. "When someone dies, they're buried in this brick section. The New Orleans sun 'bakes' them for a year and a day. After that time, only the bones are left. The bones are pushed into this section." She taps the white section. "They're piled on top of previous bones. That's how we fit so many people. People are still being buried here today."

Turn the page.

The air turns suddenly cold. Your sister yelps.

"What happened?" you ask.

"Someone tapped me on the shoulder," she says. "But there's no one there."

"Some of you will have a peaceful tour tonight," Misette says. "Others will attract ghosts without even trying." Misette's eyes narrow at you. She continues. "So, if you want to change your mind, now is the time. You can wait at the café across the street."

"I don't like the way she's looking at us," your sister says. "Let's leave."

You're not ready to leave, but your sister is clearly rattled. You bet you could convince her to stay if you tried. What do you do?

- To leave the tour, go to the next page.
- To persuade your sister to stay, turn to page 23.

"Please," your sister begs. "This is spookier than I expected."

You're disappointed, but you agree. You meet your parents at the café and order sodas.

Misette takes the remaining tourists deeper into the cemetery just as the sun goes down. Street lamps glow a dull yellow as the sky quickly turns dark. Part of you wishes you could've kept going. Suddenly, something brushes your leg. You jump!

"What?" Your sister shrieks.

"Sorry," you say, looking down. "There's a cat under my seat."

You reach down to scratch the head of a black cat, but it moves out of your reach. The cat saunters away, flicking the white tip at the end of its tail. Then it turns its head to look straight at you.

Turn the page.

"Meow!" The pitiful sound pulls at your heartstrings.

"I think the cat is lost," you say.

You watch as it heads across the street. You feel a strong urge to follow it. Your family is deep in conversation with some other tourists. No one will notice if you slip away for a little while. What do you do?

- To follow the cat, go to the next page.
- To stay with your family, turn to page 28.

"I'll be right back," you whisper to your sister. "I want to see if that cat had a collar on. I could catch it and call its owner."

The cat has crossed the street. It walks along the white wall. You stay several yards behind it. Around the corner, the wall is made of exposed brick. There's a crooked gate with a large padlock hanging to one side. The cat slides through easily and disappears.

You strain your eyes to search for the cat in the growing darkness. You're about to give up and head back to the café when you see a flicker of white.

The cat meows and flashes its eyes. They're red and glowing! It must be the weird lighting here. Curiosity gets the better of you, so you follow it.

Turn the page.

You squeeze through a gap in the gate. All around you are tombstones of different sizes and shapes. Most look like they've been here for years. Several are crumbling. Statues of angels, crosses, or birds grace the tops of some.

You zigzag through the graves, chasing the cat. At one point, you trip and fall onto your knees. When you look up, there's a man standing at the end of the path. He's tall, and his blue eyes catch the moonlight. You're so startled, you think it's a ghost. Or perhaps it's just one of the tourists who was in your group.

- To speak to the man, go to the next page.
- To run from the man, turn to page 29.

"I'm fine!" you say. "Just scraped my knees."

The man shakes his head but doesn't approach to help. "Have you seen it?" he asks. "I need to rest."

"Seen what?" you ask, standing up.

"My tombstone," he says. "Where is it? I need rest!" He repeats the questions until he's practically yelling at you.

Then he moves closer. But he's not walking towards you—he's floating! Your heart is racing.

"My name is Henry Vignes," he moans. "Have you seen my family's tomb?"

Your legs tremble. Do you help him, or do you run?

- To help the ghost, turn to page 20.
- To run, turn to page 30.

You're terrified. At the same time, you feel sorry for this poor ghost.

"I'll help you. Just don't hurt me," you say.

"Thank you," he says, "I need to find the tombstones with my family's name."

Henry floats ahead, while you stay a few steps behind. As you move through the labyrinth of tombstones, he explains his history.

"My family had a tomb here. While I was away on the high seas, my landlady kept the papers proving the tomb was mine. But she sold it to strangers, and I couldn't get it back. When I died, I was buried in an unmarked grave. But people knew my name. Is my name not written on a stone somewhere? Please help me. Do you see it?"

Your heart breaks for this ghost. How awful to cheat a person out of their final resting place. You want to help him. The cat slinks between you and Henry and heads across an open area between two large tombstones.

"Maybe the cat can help," you suggest.

Henry shakes his head. "That cat is looking for its owner. He's as lost as I am."

The cat stops, red eyes glaring at you. A small shiver runs through you.

Henry flaps his arms. "I will never find it," he roars, growing angry. "I am so very tired."

You feel hopeless. It's dark in the cemetery. The words on many tombs are faded. The stone and brick have rotted. You might have walked right by his tomb and not known it.

Turn the page.

"I'm so sorry!" you say.

Henry flies at you, fast. You step back and stumble, landing on your bottom. You raise your arms to block your face and hope for the best. *Whoosh!* Henry flies right through you.

When you open your eyes, you catch a glimpse of Henry heading off to where you first met him. You were never going to be able to help him.

Suddenly, the cat appears at your feet. It turns away and flicks its tail again.

"All right, I'll come with you," you say, as you get to your feet. "Will you take me to the exit?"

- Turn to page 26.

"Don't wimp out," you tell your sister. "We'll never get another chance like this."

Your sister sighs. "Ugh, you're right," she says.

Everyone walks one-by-one through the narrow cemetery gate. You are at the back of the group. Statues of angels and crosses sit atop some of the tombstones. You read the names of the people who are buried there. Some names are faded. Others are gone altogether.

Occasionally, someone stumbles on the path in the dark. Their yelp makes you jump. But by the third one, you almost expect it.

That's when *you* trip and fall. You land on your knees. Misette is explaining the history of the cemetery, so everyone's attention is on her. The group moves on without you. Even your sister doesn't see you.

Turn the page.

You rub your sore knees and start to get up. A flicker of white catches your attention. It's a cat—a black one. Only the tip of its tail is white. It curls and uncurls, like a finger beckoning you to follow it.

"Here, kitty!" you say.

When the cat looks at you, its red eyes glow in the moonlight. A shiver runs through you. No living cat would have eyes like that!

You try to find the tour group. You can't see them, but surely, they can't be far off. The cat reappears in front of you. It weaves in and out between your legs. You don't feel it as it curls around your leg.

"It's a ghost cat!" you say. But there's no one around to hear you.

You want to run and tell your sister. The cat meows pitifully, and something about the way its tail flickers piques your curiosity.

Suddenly, you catch a glimpse of the tour group. Your sister is beckoning you to rejoin them. But you feel like the cat is trying to show you something. Do you follow it?

- To leave your sister and follow the cat, turn to page 26.
- To ignore the cat and rejoin the group, turn to page 32.

The cat leads you into a clearing. There's a narrow path that leads up to a huge tombstone. The cat sits at the base of that monument and stares at you.

As you get closer to this tombstone, the air grows cold. Something feels seriously wrong here.

There's something different about this grave. It's a brick tombstone, and several bricks at the back of it have been broken off. In fact, it looks like it's been vandalized. People have drawn x's on every side. The x's are in groups of three. Strings of beads hang off the corners of the concrete tomb.

Along the bottom, people have placed flowers, bottles of water, and what looks like homemade crafts. No other tomb is decorated like this. Something at the top of the tombstone moves.

"Come, kitty," you say. But it isn't the cat. It's a snake! You hate snakes more than you fear ghosts.

Marie Laveau's tomb

- To run away from the snake, turn to page 33.
- To be brave and stay, turn to page 34.

27

You resist the urge to follow the cat and stay with your family for the rest of the evening. Two hours later, the tour group emerges from the cemetery. Two tourists look particularly pale. When you ask how it was, most say it was interesting, but nothing strange happened to them. But the two pale ones don't speak at all.

"We just want to go home," one says. The other simply bursts into tears.

"What happened?" you ask again.

The tour guide smiles. "If you want to know, you should come inside next time."

THE END

To follow another path, turn to page 8.
To learn more about haunted cemeteries, turn to page 103.

First the creepy cat, and now this man seems to appear out of nowhere. You can't take any more fright. You turn and run away from him.

You run toward the streetlights and away from the darkness of the cemetery. You can almost see your family at the café when your foot catches on something. You fall and slam your head on a stone slab.

When you wake up, you're in a hospital bed. Your parents and sister are relieved.

"A tour guide found you knocked out cold in the cemetery," your mother says.

"What happened?" Your dad asks.

"I . . . I don't know," you reply. All you remember is a pair of glowing red eyes. Or were they blue?

THE END

To follow another path, turn to page 8.
To learn more about haunted cemeteries, turn to page 103.

This is a real, live ghost! You run for the gate, knocking into several tombstones along the way. You don't look behind you. Henry may be following.

In the dark, you take a wrong turn. You stop to get your bearings. Which way is out? You remember a tomb with a statue of an angel. But there are so many angels. Which one is the right one?

Out of the corner of your eye, you spot a flicker of white. The cat! Instinctively, you follow it.

"How do I get out of here?" you wonder aloud.

Strangely, the cat turns to look at you. It's eyes glow bright red now. Another ghost!

What was it Misette said earlier? The living get lost here, but the ghosts know their way around. Maybe this strange cat can lead you out.

"Please help me," you repeat.

You follow the cat. With each turn, you're afraid you're going deeper into the cemetery. Finally, you spy the gate!

You squeeze your way through and dash across the street. Your family is still deep in conversation with their new friends.

"I saw a ghost!" you say, out of breath.

Your sister stares at you for a long second. Then everyone bursts out laughing.

"Good one," she says.

THE END

To follow another path, turn to page 8.
To learn more about haunted cemeteries, turn to page 103.

You don't want to get lost in this creepy place, so you rejoin the group. Misette knows a lot about the history of this cemetery. She tells of lost souls and a voodoo queen. Your sister holds on to your hand all night. Other than the occasional cold breeze, nothing exciting happens. You're a bit disappointed.

When you leave the cemetery, you look back one last time. The cat with the red eyes glares at you. You'll never know what it wanted to show you.

THE END

To follow another path, turn to page 8.
To learn more about haunted cemeteries, turn to page 103.

Ghosts you can handle, but snakes creep you out. You take off on a jog. Not too far away, you come upon a shaking young man. He's cowering on the ground.

"Are you okay?" you ask.

"The voodoo queen," he mutters. "A stupid dare. I shouldn't have come. Shouldn't have come."

You put your arm around the young man and walk him out of the cemetery. You're glad you left when you did.

THE END

To follow another path, turn to page 8.
To learn more about haunted cemeteries, turn to page 103.

The snake's head hangs off a small ledge at the top of the tombstone. Its forked tongue flickers at you. Just like the cat, this creature has red, glowing eyes.

You can barely catch a breath. You want to run, but you're frozen in place. The snake's thick body slithers down the side of the tomb and onto the ground. It slides over the gifts at the foot of the grave, right past you. Your eyes follow it.

Just beyond the tombstone is the ghost of an old woman. She wears a red and white turban on her head. A colorful shawl is draped over her shoulders.

The snake curls itself at her feet. She stares at you and frowns. Before you can take a breath, the ghost lets out a low growl. The snake wraps itself around her waist as she moves toward you. The woman swishes past you, pinching and shoving you. As she disappears, her laughter echoes in the night. You're frozen in fright. How could a ghost touch you?

You're relieved when the tour group appears. Misette looks at you knowingly.

"Did you see her?" Misette asks. "Did you see our voodoo queen?"

You nod. "Sssss-snake . . . ," you stammer.

Turn the page.

She claps her hands. "Wonderful!" she exclaims. "You're so lucky. You saw Marie Laveau. She was a greatly respected voodoo practitioner in the 1800s. People would come to her for help and spells. Even after her death, they draw three x's on her grave and beg her for help. You see all these gifts here?" The guide points to the flowers and paper crafts. "When their requests are granted by her spirit, people bring her gifts to thank her. She's not the nicest ghost, but if you've seen her, it means you will have great luck."

You're not so sure about that. It takes all your strength to follow the group back out to the café where your parents wait. They are eager to hear about your experience, but you don't have the words to describe what happened to you.

THE END

To follow another path, turn to page 8.
To learn more about haunted cemeteries, turn to page 103.

CHAPTER 3
AOYAMA CEMETERY

It's springtime in Tokyo, and the cherry blossoms are in full bloom. You're going to join your aunt and uncle on a ghost-hunting adventure during your trip. Your parents and sister think it's a weird hobby. But you're excited, and Roger and Therese are thrilled you want to join them. They insist on showing you the cemetery on your way home from the airport.

The cemetery is a beautiful place. Large walkways run between rows of tombstones. Cherry trees line both sides, and it feels as if you're walking under pink clouds.

Turn the page.

"The cemetery opened in the 1870s. Over 100,000 dead are buried here," Roger says. "This is the best place for ghost activity"

"It's also the first cemetery to have Japanese people and foreigners buried in the same place," Aunt Therese adds.

You head home with Roger and Therese to gather up their equipment. They've been given permission to camp overnight at the cemetery. But when you hop into the taxi that night, the driver refuses to take you there.

"Years ago, a driver drove past the cemetery," he said. "A woman was walking along, soaking wet. He pitied her and stopped to pick her up. She got in and sat quietly. When he looked back, the seat was wet, but the girl was gone. When I heard that, I swore never to drive that route again, bur I'll take you to the bus stop nearby."

The driver drops you off at the bus stop. You lug some camping gear and follow Roger and Therese. The sun has finally set, but the moon is full. The pinkish-white cherry blossoms brighten the area, as do the lights from the tall buildings nearby.

"This is a good place to camp," Roger says, setting down his equipment under a large tree.

You count two cameras with long lenses, a sound recording device, flashlights, and a couple of other things that look strange.

"What are those?" you ask.

"That's a thermal imaging camera," Roger says, picking up what looks like a thick magnifying glass. "It senses heat or cold."

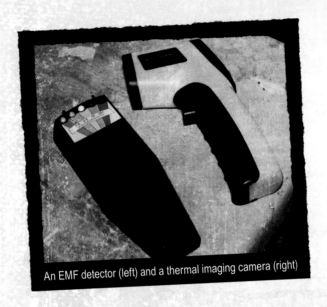
An EMF detector (left) and a thermal imaging camera (right)

"And this is an electromagnetic field or EMF detector," Therese adds. "It picks up unusual radiation. These are all to help us find ghosts."

You're thrilled that there are scientific ways to find ghosts.

"This will be our meeting place," Roger says after setting up the tent. "If we get separated, come here and wait."

Leaving the campsite, Roger has a camera in one hand and the EMF detector in the other. Therese has her recording device and imaging camera. You hang on to extra batteries and a spare camera.

"What are we looking for?" you ask.

"Anything unusual," Roger says. "A feeling, a smell, a sound that might be considered strange."

You suddenly feel like you've stepped into a large refrigerator for a moment. You shiver, but Roger and Therese don't seem to notice. Maybe you're imagining it.

You follow your uncle and aunt deeper into the cemetery. The tombstones are mostly low and neatly arranged but tightly packed. The inscriptions are in Japanese, so you can't read them, but you wish you could.

Turn the page.

There are a lot of trees and bushes in between the graves. It looks more like a peaceful park than a cemetery.

Then you notice something behind a tombstone. It's a little brown and white dog with the cutest face.

"Uncle—" you say.

"Shh!" he hisses. "We're focusing. There seems to be some presence up ahead."

He and Therese move forward quickly. You look at the dog. It's now sitting in front of a tombstone and wagging its tail at you.

Do you follow Roger and Therese, or do you go greet the pup?

- To greet the dog, go to the next page.
- To follow Roger and Therese, turn to page 52.

You'll catch up with Roger and Therese later. You step off the path toward the dog.

"Here, puppy," you say, reaching a hand toward the dog.

It wags its tail and whines. You crouch down low so as not to scare it.

"Come here," you say.

The dog yips and runs away. It might be lost and need help, so you follow it. It zips through the tombstones with ease. You try not to step on vases and flower bouquets left at the tombs.

Soon, you reach a clearing. Ahead, you see a bamboo fence held up by several stone pillars. Inside, there looks to be a small house-shaped tomb beside a larger prism-shaped one. There's a long inscription on one of the pillars.

Turn the page.

Hachikō Statue in Tokyo, Japan

You hear the dog whine, but you can't see it anywhere. You step inside the fenced-in area and look down at the tiny house grave. There's a statue of a dog in front of it—just like the dog you've been following!

A chill runs through you. Could it have been a ghost dog? It takes you a moment to come back to your senses. Flowers and gifts are scattered at the front of this grave. You crouch down to examine them. You pick up a note that is written in English. In the moonlight, you read what it says.

"A gift for Hachikō, the most loyal dog ever. You waited at the train station for your master every day after work, even after he died. For nine years, you returned to the station. I hope you have found him now, as you have crossed the rainbow bridge."

You stare at the statue of the little dog. It was his ghost that you saw.

"I hope you've found peace," you say to the statue.

Realizing that your uncle and aunt must be looking for you, you retrace your steps as best you can. But you can't find them anywhere.

What do you do?

- To go back and wait at the campsite, turn to page 48.
- To keep looking for Roger and Therese, turn to page 56.

Roger said that all the walkways lead back to the entrance, which is where your campsite is. You'd better do as he told and meet back there.

Once again, as you reach the campsite, the temperature drops. And again, you shiver.

Suddenly, your attention is drawn to something eerie. About fifty yards ahead, a girl in a white gown is walking toward you. She has long, black hair that covers her face. She looks like she's been soaked in the rain. Only, it hasn't rained all day.

You swallow. Is this the girl the taxi driver was talking about? She sounds like she's crying. And she's getting closer to you. You're filled with dread. Do you stay and see what happens? Or do you run?

- To confront the ghost, go to page 50.
- To run, turn to page 60.

The ghost dog wasn't so bad. Maybe this girl looks more terrifying than she really is. You might even be able to help her.

You try not to let your fear take control. You keep your eyes on the approaching specter.

"Hello," you say. "Do you need something? Can I help you?"

Then you notice something strange. She isn't walking to you, really. It's more of a glide. As she gets closer, you can hear her sobbing. You wonder if there's something you can do to help.

"Are you okay?" you ask.

The girl stops in her tracks. She raises her head. Her hair is still heavily draped over her face. Her sobs halt. Clearly, she's noticed you. And she knows you can see her.

You're not sure if it's real or a trick of the moonlight, but her color seems to turn green. The ghost moves again, but instead of gliding, she's hopping. It's a weird movement, and you can't decide if it's funny or scary.

- To get away from the ghost, turn to page 63.
- To stay and see what happens, turn to page 64.

"Aunt Therese, there's a dog over there," you say, hoping they'll stop.

Roger waves his hand without turning around. "It's probably a stray, not an unusual thing to find at a cemetery. We should focus on taking readings instead."

You walk all the way down this walkway. With the battery packs tucked under your arms, you scuttle behind them. You don't want to be left behind. This may be a pretty cemetery, but it's creepy too.

Roger and Therese point their instruments at different graves. Sometimes, the EMF detector makes clicking sounds, and its lights blink. Therese gets excited and mumbles something about magnetism.

Turn the page.

Roger films every step of his walk through the tombs. "This special lens can see in the dark," he explains. "Once or twice, we've seen things with the camera that our eyes didn't see."

You all tread quietly through tombstones, hoping to see or hear something. As you pass a small tomb with a bamboo fence around it, Therese swears her recording device has picked up the sound of a dog whining. But none of the other equipment registers anything unusual.

A breeze blows, making you shiver. Somewhere in the distance, a child is giggling. The cherry blossoms rain down on you. You look up and laugh too. You try to catch as many flowers as you can.

"Shh!" Therese orders.

That's when you all hear the giggle again. It came from behind you. Roger whips his camera around. Therese slips on her headphones, pointing the microphone in that direction.

The giggling stops. Roger runs down the path to try to record more and comes back looking somewhat pleased.

"I lost it," he says, "But something was there. Let's keep going."

You're getting a little bored and very sleepy.

- To stay with your aunt and uncle, turn to page 68.
- To go back to camp and sleep, turn to page 71.

You look around at the tombstones nearby. Most are dark grey with black inscriptions in Japanese on the front. You meander through several rows and come across some tombs with European names. These must be the foreigners Aunt Therese was talking about.

You wander for quite a while, and nothing happens. You feel more relaxed now.

A breeze blows through the trees, and it begins to rain cherry blossoms. You try to catch them as they fall, and you laugh out loud. Someone else laughs too.

You look around. There's no one there.

"Hello?" you call. There's no reply.

A laugh rises into the air again. It sounds like a child.

You swallow and start to walk the other way. You almost bump right into him.

About ten feet away from you stands a little boy. He's Japanese and dressed in old-fashioned clothing. He holds blossoms in his cupped hands as he giggles.

You freeze. The fact that you can see through him makes it clear that he's a ghost, but is he a friendly one?

He looks up at you. At first, he's smiling. Then his features melt like candle wax until there's nothing left. You're horrified.

The ghost rises off the ground, until he's hovering over you. Then his mouth reappears. It grows wider than his whole face. His mouth is a huge black hole, and it's coming for you.

Turn the page.

You step back and trip over something. You land on your back and scream. The last thing you see is the large black hole engulfing you.

When you wake up, it's morning, and you're back at the campsite. Roger and Therese hover over you.

"We found you in the walkway," Roger says. "I carried you back here."

It takes a few minutes to remember what happened. When you do, you tell them all about it.

Therese shakes her head. "I don't know how that happened. We didn't pick up anything at all last night. I'm glad you're safe."

THE END

To follow another path, turn to page 8.
To learn more about haunted cemeteries, turn to page 103.

You don't wait to find out if she's a good or evil ghost. You turn and run the other way. You know you're heading away from where Roger and Therese will be looking for you. But you're too scared to look back.

It seems to take forever to run the length of the walkway. When you near the end, there's a man standing at the exit. He is Japanese, but he wears a suit, tie, and hat that look more western. He's waving his arms above his head. Maybe he'll be able to help you.

You call out as you jog toward him. He shouts something in a language you don't understand and keeps waving his hands.

As you get near him, you realize he hasn't moved. He's shouting the same words over and over and waving his arms. Suddenly, moonbeams light up the park, and you see him more clearly.

He has no face under that hat. And the light shines right through him. Another ghost!

Fear freezes you in place. The ghost in front of you seems to be growing larger. You whip around and see that the girl ghost is gaining on you. How will you escape two ghosts at once?

You scream, "Uncle Roger! Aunt Therese!"

In an instant, both ghosts disappear. Your aunt and uncle come running toward you. You tell them what happened, but they're more concerned about taking readings with their equipment than they are about you. It takes several minutes before they return to your side.

"I found nothing," Therese says.

"Me neither," Roger sighs. "I believe you saw something. I just wish we had recorded it."

Turn the page.

For the rest of the night, you stick near your uncle and aunt. They're disappointed not to encounter any more ghosts. But you're not.

THE END

To follow another path, turn to page 8.
To learn more about haunted cemeteries, turn to page 103.

You're feeling less sympathetic to this ghost and more terrified. You run until you see a Japanese man in a suit. It looks a little old-fashioned, but you don't pay much attention.

"Help! Sir, there's a ghost," you cry. You don't know what you expect him to do about it, but it's comforting to see another person right now.

The man turns to look at you. As he does, the moonlight shines right through his body. The world goes black, and you pass out.

THE END

To follow another path, turn to page 8.
To learn more about haunted cemeteries, turn to page 103.

Hop. Hop. Hop.

With each hop, she's closer to you. This green, ghostly creature is almost within touching distance. That's when she stops. Her hair parts, and you see her hideous face. She has eyes black as the night and skin as pale as the moon. She glares at you and then opens her mouth. Instead of teeth, she has fangs!

She makes the most horrible sound you've ever heard. It's a cross between a scream and a laugh. You run faster than you ever have in your life. But she's fast. You barely run a few yards when she's practically on top of you.

Your foot catches on a stone, and you fall forward. You roll over just in time to see the ghost pounce on you. You scream.

The ghost freezes about two feet from you. She hovers in the air, as if frozen in place. You hear footsteps running to you. You take one last look at the ghost as she vaporizes into thin air.

By the time Therese and Roger reach you, you're panting on the ground.

"Are you all right?" Therese asks, worried.

Turn the page.

"What happened?" Roger is already scanning the area with his camera. He's filming just in case he catches proof of a ghost.

You tell them about the dog and the girl in white. Roger and Therese spend the rest of the evening taking readings of the area, the whole walkway you ran down, and the tomb of the ghost dog. They get a few strange EMF readings. Therese's equipment picks up what sounds like a dog whining.

"I've got some interesting recordings here," Therese says, excited. "I just wish we had more."

"There's nothing left here," Roger adds. "The EMF readings have stopped."

"I think my screams chased them away," you say. You're secretly glad of that.

You all spend the night back at the campsite. The next morning, you return home. After a good nap, you wake and wonder if perhaps you imagined it all. Because if you didn't, why did it only happen to you?

THE END

To follow another path, turn to page 8.
To learn more about haunted cemeteries, turn to page 103.

You walk in between tombstones, stepping over flowers, vases, and gifts left at the graves. Therese signals to you to come into a clearing.

You're in a cemented area with three tombstones scattered about. The area is surrounded by a low fence, also made of cement. Dried, rotted flowers sit in vases at the base of each grave. It looks like they haven't been visited in a while.

You hop up on the fence and watch your aunt and uncle as they take more readings. Out of the corner of your eye, you see the dog again. You wish you had the courage to follow him.

As more blossoms float down into your open hands, you think you hear someone crying.

"Do you hear that?" you ask Roger and Therese.

"Point this toward any sound you hear," Aunt Therese says, handing you the recording device. You're proud to be treated like a fellow ghost hunter and not a kid.

Sometime after midnight, just as you start to get tired, Roger gasps. You turn to look at what he sees. Three tiny orbs of light float just beyond the trees. They dance like tiny fairies, weaving in and out of the blossom-filled branches.

Turn the page.

"I knew this was a good place to hunt," Therese says. "You must have brought us good luck."

You're excited that you got to see something unusual, even if the lights aren't what you think of as ghosts. Roger explains that the electromagnetic field around those lights mean that they're not natural. "They could be spirits roaming the earth," he says.

Just before morning, the hunt ends. You help Roger and Therese pack up the campsite and head home. You collapse into bed and dream of a girl in a white dress and a little boy catching flowers falling from the trees.

THE END

To follow another path, turn to page 8.
To learn more about haunted cemeteries, turn to page 103.

"I'm really tired," you say to your aunt and uncle. "Do you two mind if I get some sleep in the tent?"

You see the disappointment on their faces.

"Wake me up if you see anything cool," you say. "I'm just exhausted from the plane ride."

"Of course," says Aunt Therese. She takes you back to the tent and says good night. You snuggle into your sleeping bag and fall asleep almost immediately. You dream you hear giggling all night.

THE END

To follow another path, turn to page 8.
To learn more about haunted cemeteries, turn to page 103.

CHAPTER 4
GREYFRIARS KIRKYARD

You haven't seen Cousin Angus in a long time, so you choose to vacation in Scotland. When you arrive, Angus tells you he fancies himself an amateur ghost hunter. He invites you to hunt with him. The adults warn you to stay away from Greyfriars, especially at night.

"Greyfriars Kirkyard is the world's most haunted cemetery," your uncle begins. "It's a terrifying place. At night, it's even worse."

Turn the page.

"Greyfriars were monks who were ordered to leave their land in 1558," Angus interrupts. He rattles on. "Mary, Queen of Scots, turned the churchyard into a cemetery. Over the years, when other cemeteries ran out of space for bodies, they were sent to Greyfriars. More bodies were dumped there from the Black Plague of 1568. More than 100,000 bodies are buried there!"

"We can take you there in the morning," your aunt says. "But best not to go after dark."

Angus turns to you and winks. That night, you're not surprised when he shakes you awake.

"What?" you mumble, opening your eyes.

It's Angus. "We're going ghost hunting."

You really like Angus, and you don't want him to think you're a baby. So you get dressed and sneak downstairs with him.

The night is clear and crisp. A few thin clouds cast shadows on the ground.

"Perfect night for ghost hunting," Angus says. He hands you a bag. In it, there are snacks, a flashlight, and a tiny yellow box. "That's a single-use film camera. If you see something unusual, take a photo. Sometimes photos pick up images we can't see."

You keep quiet. The closer you get to the graveyard, the more frightened you become.

"Here we are," Angus announces.

You look around. When did you enter a cemetery? It looks like a park with a long path down the middle. There are old brick buildings on one side and scattered tombstones on the other. Even with only the moon to light your way, this place looks peaceful.

Turn the page.

When you shine your flashlight on the buildings, you realize that they're actually graves. The dates are from the early 1600s.

You follow Angus down the path. You walk under a brick arch and come to a black iron gate. Angus shakes it.

"It's locked," you say. "Let's go a different way."

"No need," Angus says, climbing the gate.

Your eyes grow wide. You don't want to get into trouble. Do you climb the gate too?

- To not climb the gate, go to the next page.
- To climb the gate with Angus, turn to page 81.

"I'm not climbing that," you say, stubbornly. "I'll wait for you here."

Angus tries to persuade you to keep going. But you don't want to get in trouble with the police if you get caught climbing the gate.

"There must be things to explore on this side of the gate," you suggest to Angus.

Turn the page.

"Fine," he says. "But the most interesting graves must be behind the gate. Why would they lock it otherwise?"

You and Angus walk along the paths outside the gated area. You stop and read several of the tombstones. Many are faded with age. Others are written in really old English, and they're hard to understand. You stop at the grave with the name Tom Riddell.

"Wait! I recognize that name," you exclaim. "It's from that book . . ."

Angus laughs. "Yes. A lot of the names on these tombs are in those books. Look, there's McGonagall's tomb."

You are amazed. You also find other names. They're all characters in your favorite book series.

Turn the page.

Sacred

to the Memory
of Thomas Riddell Esq.
of Befsborough,
in the County of Berwick
who died in Edinburgh
on the 24. Novm. 1806,
aged 72 years.

ALSO

of Thomas Riddell Esq. his Son,
Captain of the 14.th Regiment,
who died at Trinadad in the West Indies
on the 16.th Septm. 1802,
aged 26 years.

AND

of Christian Riddell,
his Daughter,
who died in Edinburgh
on the 20. Oct. 1808,
aged 21 years.

ALSO

Maria Jane Riddell,
his daughter
died 5.th Sept. 1819
aged 47.

You stop at a wide wall with a plaque of words you can't read. Angus begins to talk about the history of the graveyard.

"This is the Covenanters wall," he explains. "These were Scottish Protestants who didn't want the King of England to interfere with their religion. They signed a document asking him to stay out. The king sent Sir George "Bloody" Mackenzie to deal with the problem. He killed 18,000 Covenanters. People called it "the Killing Time." So many were tortured and killed during this time. And they're buried here. Imagine how many ghosts there could be."

You shiver. Maybe it was a mistake to come tonight.

- To keep following Angus, turn to page 90.
- To make Angus take you home, go to page 93.

You came all the way to Scotland, so you might as well have an adventure. You climb the gate easily and land on the other side.

"The cemetery is open twenty-four hours a day," Angus says. "Except for this part. There's been a lot of vandalism here, so they lock this part up."

You walk down a stone path. Angus leads you to an old, run-down mausoleum. It has a domed roof and a heavy black door. Iron gates are locked to keep out visitors.

"This is it," Angus says. "This is Bloody George's mausoleum."

"Who?" you ask.

Angus tells you the history of the graveyard.

Turn the page.

Sir George Mackenzie's mausoleum

"Earlier, we passed the Covenanters wall. Covenanters didn't want the King of England to interfere with their religion. They signed a document asking him to stay out. The king sent this man, Sir George "Bloody" Mackenzie to deal with them. He tortured and killed 18,000 Covenanters. They're buried here."

Angus continues. "In the late 90s, a homeless man broke in. He must have awakened the spirits, because he ran out with deep scratches. They say there's an angry poltergeist in there."

"I think we should leave," you say. You're not keen on meeting the spirit of an angry ghost.

Angus calls after you, but you walk away. You turn a corner and see a man waving at you at the end of the pathway. Who else would be out at this time of night?

Turn the page.

Maybe it's a security guard. You keep walking toward him, hoping you're not in trouble.

The closer you get, the more this man looks like a shadow to you. Your steps slow. Suddenly, the shadow flies at you. You cover your face and scream.

Something bumps you, pushing you backward. How can a ghost touch you? Was it just a strong gust of wind? As you lie on the cold ground, everything goes black for a moment. Then you blink and see your cousin's face looking down at you.

"What are you doing?" he asks, puzzled.

"A-a-ghost," you stutter. "It ran through me, I think."

"Cool! What did it look like?" he asks.

Angus isn't scared, which annoys you. He helps you up and fires question after question at you. You don't want to talk about it.

"I want to go home now," you say.

"Please stay," Angus begs. He raises a large tool in his hand. "I found a wire cutter leaning against a wall. We can use it to open up Bloody George's mausoleum."

Have you had enough of this ghostly experience, or do you want the adventure to continue?

- To break into the tomb, turn to page 86.
- To make Angus take you home, go to page 93.

You head back to the mausoleum with Angus. The danger thrills you.

"I heard a couple kids took George's skull out and played ball with it," Angus says. "That's why they started locking it."

"No wonder the ghost is so mad," you say.

It takes both of you to use the cutter to break open the padlock. You're sweating by the time you finally do.

The room is dark, and it smells old and musty. You and Angus shine your flashlights around the room. Your flashlight catches a man's face. You shriek and jump back.

Angus laughs. "That's just a statue," he says.

You sigh in relief, but then the statue winks at you. Terrified, you turn and run for the door, but it shuts, locking you inside.

"Angus!" you yell. He's hopping from one foot to another.

"Something is biting me!" he screams.

Something smacks you on the head and shoves you against the wall. You wince in pain.

Turn the page.

"It's a poltergeist!" Angus howls. "Let's get out of here!"

You both tug at the heavy iron door. Something pinches your back. And the door won't budge.

"We're sorry we disturbed you," shouts Angus. "Please let us go!"

After what seems like forever, the door budges. Slowly, it opens just enough for you and Angus to squeeze through. You run to the left, and Angus runs to the right. You're both screaming.

As you run, something flies over your head, shrieking. You push yourself faster. You take whatever path you can find, ducking in between large tombstones. You finally crouch behind a statue of an angel. Maybe this will protect you.

You look up. The shadow above you looks like a giant shapeless kite. It moans and shrieks as it searches for you. You hold your breath.

A scream in the distance takes your attention away from the ghost above. That sounds like Angus. Your cousin needs you, but you're too scared to move from this hiding place. What do you do?

- To stay until the ghost disappears, go to page 95.
- To rescue Angus, go to page 97.

"And ironically, Sir George is buried here too," Angus continues. "His tomb is the one I really want to see. But it's behind that gate."

"Maybe after the sun rises," you say. "When the gate is opened."

You walk past a monument locked behind another gate. On the far wall is a tall plaque and a bust of a man. Dried leaves carpet the ground.

You turn toward the next exhibit and hear leaves rustle, but it's not at all windy. You look back at the tomb. The leaves have been brushed over to one side. The ground is wet. But it hasn't rained today.

You peer through the gate. The leaves suddenly rise up and twirl into a mini tornado. You step back. There's still no breeze blowing. How is this happening?

The leaves twirl and spin. Then they cross out of the gate and rush right at you. It's too late to run. The funnel of leaves hits you hard.

"Ouch! Stop!" you yell, to no avail.

"What's happening?" Angus asks, running to you. Suddenly, the leaves fall to the ground. Your cousin finds you standing in a pile of leaves.

"I don't know," you answer. "The leaves just flew at me."

"I think we should leave," you insist. You've had enough. You don't need to see more. "The sun is almost up. I don't want my parents to know we snuck out."

Angus reluctantly agrees. You're both back in bed within the hour, just before your parents come into your room to wake you for the day.

Turn the page.

When they ask you if you'd like to see the famous cemetery, you say no. You never want to go back there again.

THE END

To follow another path, turn to page 8.
To learn more about haunted cemeteries, turn to page 103.

Angus grumbles all the way home. He can't believe you were that close to the famous tomb and didn't go inside.

"I'll have to find someone braver next time," he says.

You get home just as your dad is walking out of the kitchen with a glass of milk.

"Where have you two been?" he says, sternly. "You're supposed to be in bed."

You and Angus explain your adventure. Your dad wakes the other adults. They are all angry that you snuck out, especially after being told not to. Your dad makes you stay in your room the rest of the day while they go sightseeing.

Turn the page.

You're secretly glad to return to your bed. Angus is mad at you, and your parents are too. It might be nice to have a quiet day to yourself. You never tell a soul about your ghostly experience, but you never forget it either.

THE END

To follow another path, turn to page 8.
To learn more about haunted cemeteries, turn to page 103.

You're frozen in place. You crouch down and hope that Angus is okay.

The ghost flutters overhead, creating a wind that whooshes around you. The temperature drops. When will this ghost give up? You cover your head and shut your eyes. You've never been so scared in your life.

Eventually, the wind dies down. You look up. The sky has cleared, and the moon is shining brightly. You take a deep breath and stand up.

The coast is clear. You run toward the sound of your cousin's scream. You find him on the ground, unconscious. His face has cuts on it.

"Angus, wake up!" You shake him, but he doesn't move.

Turn the page.

You dig through his backpack and find his cell phone. You know you're going to get in trouble, but you have to call your aunt.

The adults arrive within minutes. They are worried and angry. Angus is rushed to the hospital. By the time you all arrive, he's awake. The doctors examine him and say he's fine, just a bit banged up.

He says he was chased by a large shadow. It scratched him and shoved him to the ground. He fainted out of fright. You can relate. Your parents don't know what to think.

THE END

To follow another path, turn to page 8.
To learn more about haunted cemeteries, turn to page 103.

Another scream rips through the air. You have to help Angus.

You gather up all your courage and run. The ghost chases you. It almost knocks you over, but you stay on your feet.

Something whips at your side. It scratches you. Then something punches you in the back, and you stumble. You scramble back onto your feet. You run past Mackenzie's mausoleum and head toward Angus. Wicked cackles fill the air.

You come to a clearing. It's a park-like setting with a few tombstones jutting up from the ground and trees scattered about. In the middle of the clearing, is Angus. He's on the ground, screaming for help.

"I'm coming!" you cry, as you dash toward him.

Turn the page.

You dive under the shadowy ghost and grab Angus by the arm. It's as windy under this ghost as it was under yours. The wind knocks you to your knees.

"Look!" Angus shouts, pointing up.

Both shadow ghosts have now merged into one gigantic cloud. How are you going to get out of this?

"We must find an angel statue," he says.

"Why?" you ask.

"They can protect us," he answers

You hope he's right. The two of you run to the nearest angel-decorated tombstone. The ghosts whip up a strong wind, but you push through.

Crouched under a large tombstone, you watch the shadows block out the moonlight. They move closer with each second. This must be how it ends for you. You shut your eyes and hope that your parents will forgive you for disobeying them.

As suddenly as it started, the wind stops. The ghosts have disappeared.

"Angus, look," you say, nudging him. "The sun has risen."

Sure enough, it's morning. The sun lights up the green grass and trees. All signs of ghosts and poltergeists have gone.

You and Angus sit silently on the damp grass for a long time. The cuts and bruises on your body ache, but other than that, you're not hurt.

Turn the page.

In silence, you both get up and walk home. When you get there, your parents are furious with you for sneaking out. For the rest of the day, you're grounded in your rooms. They're mad enough already. You can never tell them what happened to you there.

THE END

To follow another path, turn to page 8.
To learn more about haunted cemeteries, turn to page 103.

CHAPTER 5
GHOSTS IN GRAVEYARDS

The supernatural has captured our imaginations and triggered our fears for all of human history. There are those who like the idea of loved ones hanging around a bit longer on Earth. And there are people who don't believe in ghosts at all.

Ghost hunters have recorded what they believe to be supernatural occurrences. They measure magnetic fields that are stronger in one place than in other places and think this means there's a ghost there.

An EMF meter

Those who don't believe in ghosts say that science can explain these experiences. Unusual magnetic readings can often be caused by Earth's magnetic field or come from large equipment in the area.

One set of experiments showed that low-frequency sound waves could cause people to feel uncomfortable and to sense something strange in the room. We can't hear the sounds, but we can see or feel the effects of it. This is what people think is the presence of a ghost.

Scientists who have studied people's brains believe that electrical stimulation can cause a person to feel someone is watching them. This could also be an explanation for a ghostly encounter.

Whether ghosts are real or not, there are some experiences that cannot be explained. And people will stand on one side or the other of the fence, sure that what they believe is the truth.

MORE GHOSTLY ENCOUNTERS

There are several haunted cemeteries in the United States. The oldest cemetery in the United States is Grove Street Cemetery in Connecticut. There are graves there that go back to the 1700s. People believe there are some very old ghosts here.

Grove Street Cemetery in Connecticut

At Union cemetery in Easton, Connecticut, there's a White Lady who roams the area. People also report having seen red eyes that peer out of a bush at them.

Visitors to the Chestnut Hill Cemetery in Exeter, Rhode Island, have reported vampires as well as ghosts.

Finally, Bachelor's Grove Cemetery in Chicago, Illinois, is a private cemetery that has a ghost dog. The big, black dog guards the entrance to the cemetery. He disappears if you get too close.

OTHER PATHS TO EXPLORE

Imagine you are an evening security guard or a caretaker of a cemetery. Do you think you would be more likely or less likely to believe in ghosts if you had to work in a dark, spooky cemetery every day? Once you got used to it, would it feel less creepy?

Let's assume ghosts are real. How or why do you think ghosts might be created? What might they want?

Imagine you have had a ghostly encounter. Would you tell anyone about it? Why or why not?

GLOSSARY

inscription (inn-SKRIP-shuhn)—writing, carving, engraving, or marking words or letters on something

interfere (in-tuhr-FEER)—to try to control the concerns of others

linger (LING-gur)—to stay or wait around

kirkyard (KERK-yahrd)—a Scottish term for churchyard, which is another term for a cemetery

mausoleum (maw-suh-LEE-uhm)—a large building that holds tombs

poltergeist (POLE-tuhr-gyst)—a ghost that causes physical events, such as objects moving

vandalism (VAN-duhl-ihzm)—intentional destruction or defacement of property

voodoo (VOO-doo)—a religion that began in Africa; voodoo is also spelled vodou

BIBLIOGRAPHY

Aoyama Cemetery: Remembrance in the Heart of Tokyo kanpai-japan.com/tokyo/aoyama-cemetery

Le Carrer, Olivier. *Atlas of Cursed Places: A Travel Guide to Dangerous and Frightful Destinations.* New York: Black Dog & Leventhal, 2015.

Pierce, Sophie. "Greyfriars Kirkyard in Edinburgh Guide – Bobby, Harry Potter & The Most Haunted Graveyard in the World!" August 2, 2023. *Third Eye Traveller.* Accessed August 25, 2023. thirdeyetraveller.com/greyfriars-kirkyard-edinburgh-haunted-bobby/

Steiger, Brad. *Real Ghosts, Restless Spirits, and Haunted Places.* Canton, MI: Visible Ink Press, 2013.

Thompson, Dave. *Haunted America FAQ: All That's Left to Know About the Most Haunted Houses, Cemeteries, Battlefields, and More.* Montclair, NJ: Backbeat Books, an imprint of Hal Leonard Corporation, 2015.

READ MORE

Dean, Jessa. *The Ghostly Tales of Sleepy Hollow.* Charleston, SC: Arcadia Children's Books, 2021.

Peterson, Megan Cooley. *Can You Escape a Haunted Battlefield?: An Interactive Paranormal Adventure.* North Mankato, MN: Capstone Press, 2025.

Troupe, Thomas Kingsley. *Haunted Graveyards and Temples.* New York: Crabtree Publishing Company, 2022.

INTERNET SITES

Haunted Tales from the Grave
travelchannel.com/interests/haunted/photos/haunted-tales-from-the-grave

St. Louis Cemetery #1
usghostadventures.com/haunted-cities/new-orleans-most-haunted/st-louis-cemetery-1/

ABOUT THE AUTHOR

Ailynn Collins learned a lot about writing from her teachers at Hamline University in St. Paul, MN. She has always loved reading science fiction stories about other worlds and strange aliens. She enjoys creating new characters and worlds for her stories, as well as envisioning what the future might look like. When not writing, Collins enjoys spending her spare time reading and playing board games with her family. She lives near Seattle, Washington, with her husband and lovable dogs.